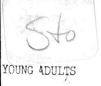

# The Western Alliance

# People, Politics and Powers

The Communist Bloc
The United Nations
Human Rights
Terrorism
The World Health Organization
Toward United Europe
The Multi-National Companies
The Western Alliance

# The Western Alliance

BRIAN RIGBY

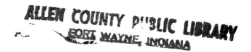
First published in 1979 by
Wayland Publishers Limited
49 Lansdowne Place, Hove
East Sussex, BN3 1HF, England

ISBN 0 85340 672 3

Phototypeset by Trident Graphics Limited, Reigate, Surrey
Printed by Gale and Polden Ltd., Aldershot,
and bound by The Western Book Company.

# CONTENTS

2085463

# Introduction: the wartime alliance

Over thirty years have gone by since a large area of Europe lay in ruins. In those years new generations have grown up who have never heard the scream of falling bombs or the thud of gunfire. This peace is a great blessing which must be constantly remembered, for it is threatened in many ways.

Between 1940 and 1945 much of Europe had been under Nazi German control. In 1942 German power extended from northern Norway to the Mediterranean coast of Africa and from the Atlantic coast of France deep into Russia. Britain had gone to war with Germany in 1939 in an attempt to prevent Germany from dominating Europe because Britain always tried to prevent any single European country from becoming too powerful.

In 1941, Hitler the German leader launched an attack on his former ally, the USSR. The British Prime Minister, Winston Churchill, said 'If Hitler invaded Hell I would make at least a favourable reference to the Devil in the House of Commons.' Churchill hated Russian Communism but he hated Nazi Germany more, so Britain and the USSR became allies. At the end of 1941 when Japan attacked the United States, the Americans joined Britain and the USSR in an alliance against Germany. This alliance came about simply because Britain, the USSR and the USA had a common enemy.

The grand alliance of three powerful countries broke the Germans. The bitter struggle probably cost the lives of over thirty million Europeans. Twenty million of these were Russian. The Russians were determined that such a disaster should never happen to them again. After the war, in July 1945, the Allied leaders met at Potsdam in Germany. They confirmed a decision reached during the war to divide Germany

*Opposite* Harry S. Truman, President of the United States from 1945 to 1952.

7

Adolf Hitler, dictator of Germany from 1934 to 1945.

and the city of Berlin into four zones to be occupied and administered by the Americans, British, French and Russians. This was to be a temporary arrangement until the Allies could set up a democratic German government. In addition, the USSR altered the map of Eastern Europe by taking in large areas of land from eight countries on her western border and moving the Polish frontier 320 kilometres westward into former German territory.

The Americans disliked the way the USSR had compensated Poland with German territory. But at this time the Americans perfected the atomic bomb (see Chapter 10) which gave them an immense military advantage. An American official tried to cheer up President Truman over Soviet policy by saying, 'Mr President, you have an atomic bomb up your sleeve.' Truman replied, 'Yes, but I am not sure it can ever be used.'

# 1  Communism and the West

The growing divisions after the Potsdam Conference are not surprising. Many ordinary people in the West were pained and annoyed at the time by what appeared to be Soviet aggressive stubbornness. During the war, the USSR had been portrayed in the West in newspapers, film and on radio as a brave and gallant ally. This had been a temporary change from earlier hostility which dated back to 1917 when the Bolshevik party in Russia seized power and transformed the country into a Communist state.

One result of the revolution was that Russia withdrew from the First World War against Germany. Naturally this angered Britain and the USA. The Communists declared they meant to bring about revolutions in all the countries of the world. They wanted to overthrow the governments of the leading capitalist countries, including Britain and the USA. The theories of Communism were preached as a new religion. They appealed to the workers in the West to clear away their kings, priests, bankers and businessmen and organize the state for their own benefit.

Fear and anger rose in the governments of the West. It was believed that Communist agents were secretly working, as Churchill said, like 'germ cells from which the cancer of Communism should grow'. From 1918 to 1920, British, American, French, Japanese, Italian and Czech troops were fighting in Russia to overthrow the Communist government. The numbers were small and the intervention failed, but the Russians never forgot what they saw as a stab in the back during a bitter civil war.

During the 1920s and 1930s both the USSR and the USA were fully occupied with their internal difficulties. Each government believed it knew the right way

to create a full and happy life for people. In the USSR, the state governed all aspects of life, and the economy was run by government planners in Moscow. In the USA the government generally left individuals and businesses to settle their own affairs. In both countries there was great economic growth which was based on their natural and human resources. Both countries were suspicious of each other's ideas and attitudes. It was the growing conflict over these ideologies that dominated the period after the Second World War.

American youth in the Cherry Blossom Parade in Washington. Miss Alaska, a beauty queen, headed the parade.

*Opposite* A procession of Soviet youths in Red Square, Moscow, in May 1978.

11

# 2 Western Alliances

As the wartime friendship grew weaker, the differences grew stronger between the USSR on the one hand and America and Britain on the other. In March 1946 Churchill said,
'From Stettin on the Baltic to Trieste on the Adriatic an iron curtain has descended across the Continent.'
He meant that the Russians would resist the effects of Western ideas and attitudes behind this 'iron curtain'.

Joseph Stalin, Russian leader from 1924 to 1953.

A US landing craft arrives at the beach at Mindoro, Philippines, in part of vast SEATO manoeuvres in 1962.

Stalin, the Russian leader, was very angry and said, 'To all intents and purposes, Mr Churchill now takes his stand among the war-mongers.' The Americans disliked the way in which the Russians set up Communist governments in Eastern Europe. They realized that Britain was no longer strong enough to exercise world leadership and that the USSR would do so if they did not act.

The first objective was to restore Western Europe's economic strength, because Communism flourished when people were poor and hungry. In June 1947, the Marshall Plan offered massive American aid to European countries. While the Western countries gratefully accepted, the USSR refused to allow the countries of Eastern Europe to come under American 'imperialistic plans of expansion'.

The economic containment of the USSR was not enough. During 1948 Americans moved towards setting up a military alliance. This became urgent when the crisis developed over Berlin in the summer of 1948 (see Chapter 4). The Americans were ready to commit their armed forces to the defence of Western Europe. In April 1949 the North Atlantic Treaty Organization was formed. The countries which joined the alliance were the USA, Britain, France, Belgium, Netherlands, Luxembourg, Italy, Iceland, Canada, Denmark, Norway and Portugal. They agreed 'that an armed attack against one or more of them in Europe or North America shall be considered an attack against them all'. The NATO alliance became the main means of Western defence and is the basis of the Western Alliance. It was expanded in 1952 to include Greece and Turkey and in 1955 to include Western Germany.

If war broke out, the small NATO ground forces – 'the shield' – were intended to delay the Soviet ground forces until 'the sword' – long range nuclear bombers – could strike at the Soviet homeland. In 1954 the Americans formed a similar alliance to stop

NATO exercise in Germany in 1969. A chieftain tank crosses rough country.

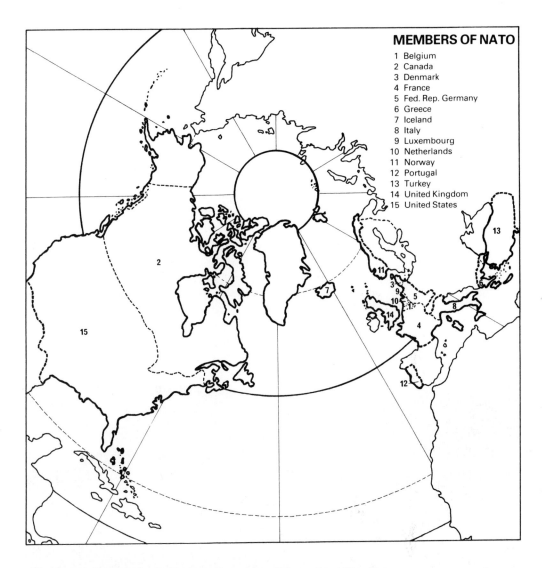

**MEMBERS OF NATO**

1 Belgium
2 Canada
3 Denmark
4 France
5 Fed. Rep. Germany
6 Greece
7 Iceland
8 Italy
9 Luxembourg
10 Netherlands
11 Norway
12 Portugal
13 Turkey
14 United Kingdom
15 United States

the spread of Communism in the Far East. The South East Asia Treaty Organization (SEATO) included the USA, Britain, France, Australia, New Zealand and three Asian countries, Pakistan, the Philippines and Thailand. This alliance was never as strong as NATO because of the great differences between the member countries. Another alliance was formed in 1955 (Baghdad Pact) between Britain, Iraq, Iran, Turkey and Pakistan. It linked NATO and SEATO and encircled the USSR with a ring of countries determined to defend themselves.

15

# 3 The Warsaw Pact

The three interlocking alliances confirmed Soviet fears of the Western allies. The Belgian government, a member of NATO, tried to reassure the Russians: 'The idea of aggression against the USSR has never been considered within the Alliance. Our plans have at all times been exclusively aimed at preventing war.' But the Russians were not impressed. They saw the growing number of American military bases round the world. It was one thing for the Americans to try to stop the spread of Communism into the Western world, but how could they be sure the Americans would not try to destroy Communism in

Warsaw Pact forces on manoeuvres. Troops rest during an interval between 'battles'.

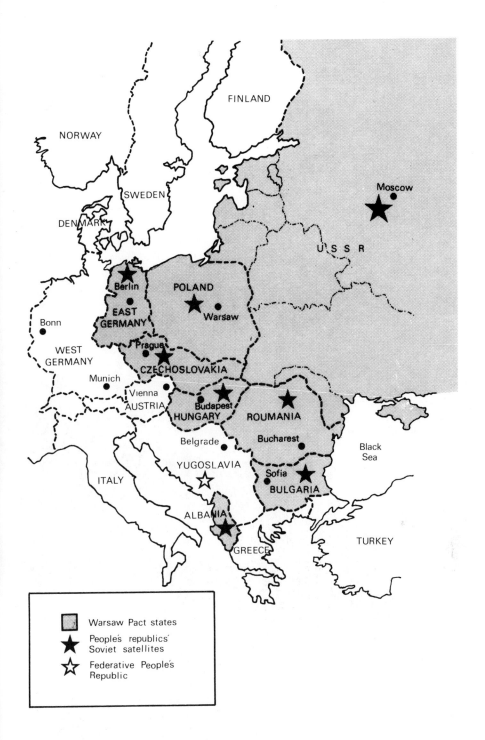

**COMMUNIST BLOC AND WARSAW PACT COUNTRIES**

Eastern Europe and in the USSR itself? According to
a Soviet history book: 'Ruling circles in the US played
the leading role in unleashing the Cold War. Having
invented tales of a "Soviet menace" and a "communist
danger", American imperialism adopted a policy of
"rolling back" communism, a policy of "liberating"
the socialist states.'

The decisive event for the USSR came when West Germany joined NATO in 1955. It was to them 'the policy of reviving German militarism'. So in May 1955, the Russians drew up their own treaty. It was the Warsaw Pact. This changed Soviet control of Eastern European countries into a treaty of 'friendship, co-operation and mutual assistance'. It was signed by the USSR, Poland, Czechoslovakia, East Germany, Hungary, Rumania, Bulgaria and Albania. Since these satellite countries had already been under Soviet control, the new treaty did not make major changes. It did give the smaller countries more say in Soviet decisions.

So two military alliances faced each other across central Europe, NATO and the Warsaw Pact. Both of them are still pledged to preserve peace and protect the liberty of the member nations. To each other, they seem aggressive. In both cases a super-power dominates the smaller countries and uses them to support its own policies and power. According to the Russians, 'The USA regarded NATO from the very outset as an important weapon for extending its influence in Western Europe.' It may be that these organizations have prevented serious disputes between their members but there are terrible dangers of an armed conflict breaking out between the alliances by accident or design.

The 'Berezina' exercises of 1978; an armour attack.

20

# 4  Germany: centre of conflict

Germany was a great problem in post-war Europe. At the end of the war, the USSR, USA and Britain decided that Germany should remain united. Very soon these intentions faded. The British and Americans gave cash and goods to revive the economy in their zones of Germany, while the Russians took goods and whole factories from their zone to compensate for the great damage caused by the Germans in the USSR. The Western Allies realized that a strong and friendly Germany would be safer in their growing enmity with the USSR than a weak Germany kept under close allied control. The Russians had no intention of giving up their control of Eastern Germany,

The Berlin Air Lift. A C-54 is loaded with coal at an airfield in Germany.

which was so important for their security. Stalin correctly predicted in 1948: 'The West will make Western Germany their own and we shall turn Eastern Germany into our own state.'

During 1947 and 1948 the British, Americans and French merged their zones. The Russians felt that the Western Allies were going to create a new West German government which would be used in an anti-Soviet alliance. They decided to try to absorb West Berlin by cutting off its supplies. The roads and railways from West Germany to West Berlin were blocked. This was the first major 'battle' in the Cold War. The Western Allies used over 500 aircraft flying night and day to supply the city with everything it

The Berlin Wall. A British delegation of Labour M.P.'s (including Harold Wilson, in the centre) inspect the wall in the Staaken sector.

23

Troops of the Welch regiment patrol a lonely part of the Berlin frontier.

Looking across towards East Berlin from Checkpoint Charlie.

needed, including coal! The Russians thought the city would be starved into surrender, but the morale of the Berliners remained high in spite of the shortages of the winter of 1948. Eventually, in May 1949, the Russians allowed supplies in by road and rail in return for the promise of a conference on Germany.

This was a victory for the West. It showed that the Western Allies were determined that West Berlin should be linked with West Germany. After elections throughout West Germany, in August the German Federal Republic was set up with its capital in Bonn.

Prosperity behind the wall. This is the building of the Foreign Ministry, East Berlin.

Soon after, in October, the German Democratic Republic was set up in East Germany. The Communist government of East Germany was not popular and in the cities in June 1953 there were serious riots, which were crushed with the help of the Soviet Army. East Germans could escape their government and country by going to West Berlin and then escaping to West Germany. Millions fled to get a better life in the West until, in 1961, the East German government set up a concrete wall to cut off West Berlin from East Berlin. This closed off the 'hole in the iron curtain'.

Germany remains a divided country today. West Germany (GFR) is one of the most important members of NATO and East Germany (GDR) is a very powerful member of the Warsaw Pact. Most Germans hope that one day their country will be united again but their governments are now so different that it would be hard to bring them together.

# 5 Soviet satellites in Eastern Europe

In Eastern Europe Stalin created an empire in which the separate countries were ruled by Communists with Soviet interests at heart. Only Yugoslavia was able to break away from the domination of Moscow, in 1948. Yugoslavia remained Communist but adapted the system to its own needs.

After Stalin died in 1953 his harsh policy was softened in the USSR by Khrushchev. The satellite countries also expected to see some relaxation of Soviet control. The Russians accepted a new leader in

The occupation of Prague, 1968. Soviet tanks roar down a street in central Prague.

28

Poland in 1956. Gomulka supported change but agreed to uphold Communism and preserve the Warsaw Pact. The discontent spread into Hungary, and there the new leader, Nagy, was unable to control the wave of anti-Communist and anti-Russian feeling which swept the country. Nagy announced in November 1956 that Hungary was leaving the Warsaw Pact and appealed for help to the United Nations. The USSR could not tolerate the possibility of Hungary becoming neutral and non-Communist. Although the Russians knew the use of force would damage their reputation, the risks of not interfering were too great. Soviet tanks smashed the uprising. Nagy was executed and over 140,000 Hungarians fled from the country before the border was sealed off.

One more brave attempt to combine Communism with individual liberty and national independence occurred in Czechoslovakia. In 1968 Alexander Dubček became Czechoslovakia's leader and started relaxing government controls. Czech newspapers, radio

Defiant Czechs jeer the passing tanks in Prague, 1968.

*Opposite* Hungary, 1956. Demonstrators dismantle the boots of a gigantic statue of Lenin.

29

An Hungarian Gestapo member shot in the streets of Budapest during the uprising of 1956.

and television discussed current affairs and criticized Soviet policies. The Russians and their allies were worried that this more democratic form of Communism might spread. In July 1968 they warned the Czechs: 'We cannot agree to have hostile forces push your country away from Socialism . . .' Dubček tried to reassure them that Czechoslovakia was loyal to the Warsaw Pact and only wanted reasonable internal changes. The Soviet leaders Kosygin and Brezhnev met Dubček and appeared to accept his policy. But a few days later, on August 21st, 1968 Czechoslovakia was invaded by her Warsaw Pact allies. The 'Prague Spring' of hope that Communism might develop a democratic form with a respect for liberty was dashed.

Western countries were shocked at the Soviet display of brute force, but they recognized that these countries were clearly in the Soviet zone of influence.

# 6 Communism in China

The Cold War developed between the Western allies and the USSR after the Second World War. It soon became a worldwide conflict, because of the Communist victory in China. After a long civil war the Chinese Communist leader Mao Tse-tung announced in October 1949 the foundation of the People's Republic of China.

The Americans backed the losing side in the civil war, the Nationalist Chinese, who fled to the island of Taiwan (Formosa) under American protection. The Americans thought that the Soviet Communists had now gained control of China, the world's largest country in terms of population, by helping the Chinese. In 1950 the USSR and China signed a treaty of friendship.

This American view was largely wrong. Stalin and his party did not want a powerful China. The long frontier between Russia and China was a breeding ground for quarrels. There were also deep differences between the two countries over the right way to organize a Communist society. As long as Stalin was alive, these differences were hidden. Mao regarded him as the leader of the Communist world, and the USSR gave China much technical help in the 1950s to build important industries. Mao disagreed with Stalin's successor, Khrushchev, who believed that Communism could triumph in the world by winning elections. Mao rejected this policy, arguing that 'the power of the gun' must be used to bring about 'violent revolution'. He felt that in any world war the West would be destroyed and that Communism would survive.

An important break between China and the USSR came in 1959. Khrushchev refused to supply China with the atomic bomb. The Chinese had to wait until

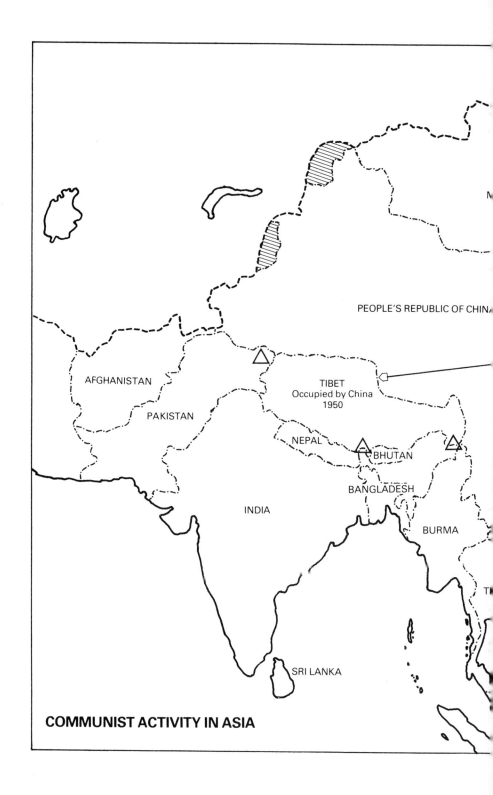

PEOPLE'S REPUBLIC OF CHINA

AFGHANISTAN

PAKISTAN

NEPAL

TIBET
Occupied by China
1950

BHUTAN

BANGLADESH

INDIA

BURMA

SRI LANKA

**COMMUNIST ACTIVITY IN ASIA**

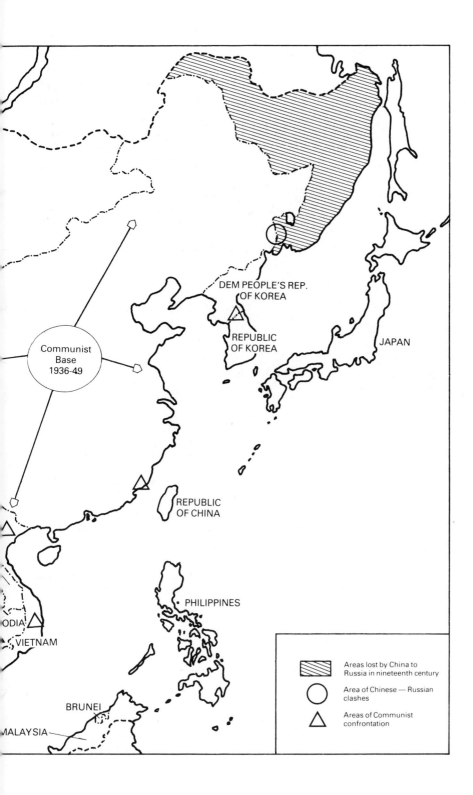

DEM PEOPLE'S REP.
OF KOREA

REPUBLIC
OF KOREA

JAPAN

Communist
Base
1936-49

REPUBLIC
OF CHINA

PHILIPPINES

ODIA

VIETNAM

BRUNEI

MALAYSIA

Areas lost by China to
Russia in nineteenth century

Area of Chinese — Russian
clashes

Areas of Communist
confrontation

Nikita Khrushchev meets Mao Tse-Tung at Peking for the Soviet Exhibition in October 1954.

1964 before they exploded their first atomic bomb. A mistrust grew between China and the USSR in the 1960s, especially as the tension between the USA and the USSR began to ease.

If the Western Alliance had not been involved in the Korean War, and the USA in Vietnam, it is possible that the West might have seen that the split between China and the USSR was deeper than the apparent common unifying factor that both had Communist governments. Throughout the 1950s and 1960s the USA saw Communism as a worldwide threat and tried to isolate China. Despite this Western hostility, the Chinese and Soviet quarrel became worse. Angry words gave way to open fighting. In 1969, Soviet and Chinese troops were killed in small clashes along the border. Both sides moved heavy reinforcements to the border areas, but then withdrew. A full-scale war would have had incalculable effects. Since then, Chinese-Soviet relationships have remained tense as both countries strive to show themselves as the true leaders of the Communist world. Their border disputes remain unresolved.

# 7 The Cold War in Asia: Korea

There was bound to be conflict in Asia between the Western Alliance and Communism. Since the nineteenth century large areas of the continent had been controlled by European powers, mainly Britain and France. The two World Wars weakened their control of countries such as India and Indo-China. After 1945 the people of Asia wanted to control their own future. As Asian countries won their independence,

British troops in winter gear in Korea.

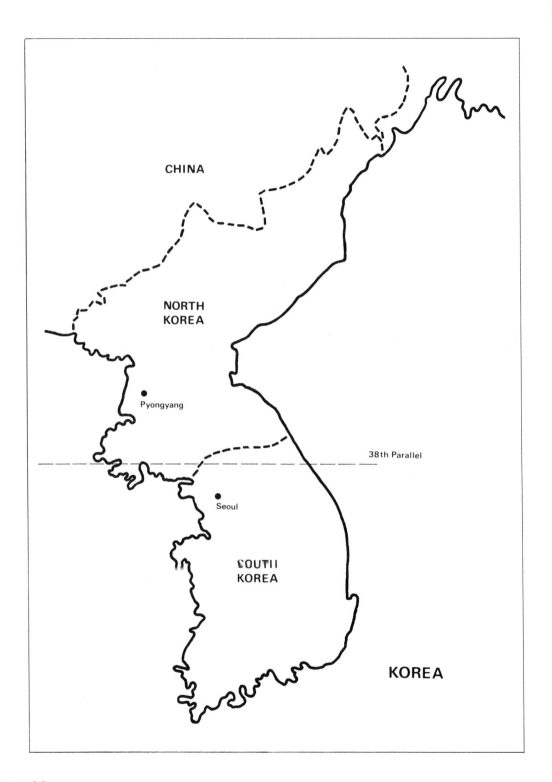

CHINA

NORTH
KOREA

● Pyongyang

38th Parallel

● Seoul

SOUTH
KOREA

KOREA

there was a great opportunity for the Communists to take over the new governments. The Communists in the USSR and in China could spread their form of government into neighbouring countries.

United Nations forces used jet fighter aircraft in their operations in Korea.

India has the highest population in Asia, after China. It became independent of British rule in 1947, along with neighbouring Pakistan. Neither country needed Communist support to win independence, but the great poverty and deprivation in both countries make them vulnerable to a Communist revolution.

Another former British colony, Malaya, had a more difficult route to independence. There were two main races in the country, the Malays and Chinese, who were often opposed to each other. In 1948 the Communist group amongst the Chinese in Malaya began a rebellion which lasted over twelve years. The rebellion was beaten by British and Malayan forces. They fought the guerillas by driving them into remote

jungle. In 1957 Malaya became independent and remained free from Communist domination.

In other countries the transition from colonial rule to independence and unity was difficult. The war in Indo-China lasted from 1945 to 1975 and in Korea there was war between the West and Communist China. The Korean War was not an independence struggle in the strict sense. Korea had been a Japanese colony until 1945, when the Japanese surrendered to the Soviet army in the northern half of Korea and the American army in the south. In the North, a Communist government was set up. An anti-Communist government was organized after elections in the South. This meant that it was impossible to unite the country as had been intended.

In June 1950 North Korean troops crossed the 38th parallel, the line dividing the North from the South. They wanted to unify the country under Communist rule. President Truman summed up American feeling by saying 'Communism has passed beyond the use of subversion to conquer independent nations and will now use armed invasions and war.' The USA asked for United Nations forces to defend South Korea. The Soviet delegate was not present, so the United Nations agreed that all members should help the South Koreans. Although many nations sent contin-

British troops build a fence to protect Chinese squatters against Communist guerrillas in Malaya, 1950.

*Opposite* A Greek soldier is decorated for his service in the Unified Forces in Korea.

A casualty is evacuated from the Malayan jungle by helicopter in 1953.

gents, the majority of fighting forces came from the USA.

The outcome of the war hung in the balance. The decisive event occurred in November 1950 as UN forces neared the Chinese border. Now a great Communist power, China entered open war with the USA. After years of bitter fighting, and five million casualties, an armistice was signed in 1953. The line between North and South Korea was left near the 38th parallel.

The Korean War showed that America would fight to control Communism even at great cost in lives and money. Asia was soon ringed by American bases and the SEATO alliance (see Chapter 2). The USA now took on the role of world policeman and China retired into isolation behind a 'bamboo curtain'.

# 8 Africa: independence and Communism

In 1945 Africa was almost completely under European control. European weapons were vastly superior to native arms, and a handful of troops could destroy whole native armies. However the same nationalist movements which had developed in Asia were also present in Africa. Africans too resented being exploited by Europeans.

Since 1945, far-reaching changes have led to the independence of all African states from European political control. These changes gave the Communists a chance to intervene.

This was particularly true in Egypt, which had to

Using loans and advisers from China, African workers build the Tanzam railway.

Soviet ships in Egypt. These mine-sweepers are working near the Egyptian harbour of Hurgada.

end British domination and fight wars with Israel. When the Egyptians took control of the Suez Canal in 1956, the British and French attacked Egypt. They used the excuse of restoring peace after Israel had invaded. This last attempt at European control was met by worldwide opposition. The USSR emerged as champions of Egypt and the Arab cause, and began to provide Egypt with massive supplies of modern military equipment and advisers. In further wars between Egypt and Israel in 1967 and 1973 the Egyptians used Soviet equipment and the Israelis used American and French equipment. But the Egyptian leader, President Sadat, had expelled Soviet advisers from Egypt in 1972. It appeared that the Russians were no more acceptable in a dominant position than the British or French had been.

The USSR suffered another setback in Zaire, formerly the Belgian Congo. When the Belgians left this immense country in 1960, the army mutinied and whites were massacred. The Belgians sent in paratroopers to restore order, but the Congolese saw this as an attempt to end independence. The leader of the mineral-rich province of Katanga, Moise Tshombe, declared his province independent. He was supported by the Belgian mining companies. The Prime Minister, Patrice Lumumba, asked for UN forces to preserve order, but he wanted to get the Belgians out. He called on the Russians to help him, and they sent advisers and fifteen planes. The US representative at the UN accused the Russians of 'trying to bring the Cold War into the heart of Africa'. But the Russians were supporting a loser. Lumumba was eventually murdered and succeeded by a soldier, Mobutu, who had Western support. Lumumba became a martyr for the Communist world.

These Communist failures may have made the Americans give a low priority to African problems. It was felt that Communism would make little progress in Africa with its tribal allegiances and largely rural population. The West was concerned, however, when

Patrice Lumumba, Nationalist leader of the Belgian Congo, assassinated in 1961.

43

The President of Katanga province in the Congo, Moise Tshombe.

Tanzania and Zambia invited the Chinese to build a railway between the two countries during 1970–1975. More problems arose in Angola and Ethiopia. Angola slipped into civil war after the Portuguese left. The pro-Communist group, the Marxist MPLA, was backed by the Russians. They supplied the MPLA with arms and ferried to Africa up to 25,000 troops from Cuba, a Communist country. These soldiers guaranteed a pro-Communist victory in Angola, and later in Ethiopia where a civil and foreign war was going on.

Africa with its vital raw materials is seen as a continent whose support cannot be taken for granted. Western countries are anxious to settle African problems, especially in southern Africa. The ending of white domination in Rhodesia might prevent further Communist successes.

# 9 Latin America: the US dilemma

Latin America – the states of Central and South America – appeared to be safe from Communist penetration in 1945. The influence of the anti-Communist Roman Catholic Church was strong; Latin America seemed to be squarely in the Western camp. But the dominance of the USA was the great danger to this position. For over a hundred years the United States had interfered in the affairs of Latin American states to suit its own needs, as when it took

The Soviet cruiser *Grozny*, flagship of a small flotilla, at Havana harbour in Cuba.

CENTRAL AND SOUTH AMERICA

USA

New York

MEXICO

Havana

BAHAMAS

CUBA
HAITI
HONDURAS
JAMAICA
DOMINICAN
REPUBLIC
PUERTO RICO

GUATEMALA
SALVADOR
NICARAGUA

COSTA
RICA

PANAMA

GALAPAGOS IS.

ECUADOR

VENEZUELA

COLOMBIA

GUYANA

PERU

BRAZIL

BOLIVIA

PARAGUAY

CHILE

ARGENTINA

URUGUAY

FALKLAND IS.

States without elected
governments

Communist states

Colonial territories

USA

National Communist movements

Severe inflation

46

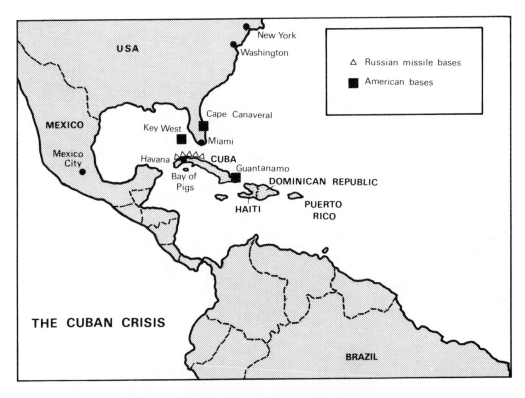

control of the Panama Canal zone. As a result, Latin American countries were suspicious of the USA.

To help the fight againt Communism, the USA was prepared to aid the overthrow of pro-Communist governments. They sent military and economic help to régimes opposed to Communism, even if they were corrupt and unpopular. In 1954 the USA engineered the overthrow of the Guatemalan government. US marines invaded the Dominican Republic in 1965 to ensure the establishment of a friendly government. These actions began to divide the Western Alliance.

President Kennedy of the USA was sensitive to these mistakes. In 1961 he declared: 'I have called on all the people of the hemisphere to join in a new Alliance for Progress . . . a vast co-operative effort . . . to satisfy the basic needs of the American people [i.e. Latin American] for homes, work and land, health and schools.' But the words were spoiled by new events in Cuba.

In 1959, a young lawyer, Fidel Castro, led a revolution to bring about social justice and economic

Fidel Castro (centre) in Red Square, Moscow, as the guest of N. Khrushchev (left), and Leonid Brezhnev (right).

growth. He took control of US business interests in Cuba, and adopted Communism. US hostility was deep and the Central Intelligence Agency supported an invasion in 1961 by anti-Castro rebels, which was destroyed on the beaches of the Bay of Pigs in Cuba.

The Soviet leader, Khrushchev, saw his opportunity. He could provide Cuba with the economic and military aid to fend off the USA. Also he could turn Cuba into a Soviet base, equipped with medium range ballistic missiles and bombers. This would enable the Russians to make a nuclear strike into the heart of the USA. In October 1962, US air reconnaissance proved that Soviet missiles were in Cuba. Kennedy broadcast to the American people: 'We will not risk prematurely or unnecessarily the course of a world-wide nuclear war . . . but neither will we shrink from that risk if at any time it must be faced.' He ordered the US fleet to blockade Cuba to prevent further military supplies from the USSR reaching the island. Khrushchev wanted to avoid nuclear war. After a week in which the world was poised on the edge of this catastrophe, the Russians agreed to remove the missiles if the USA promised not to invade Cuba.

Cuba tried to spread Communism to other Latin American countries. The USA was still ready to intervene, usually indirectly, to protect its position. In Chile in 1970 a Marxist government led by President Allende was elected. It had Communist backing, and took control of the American-owned copper mines. It is widely believed that once again the American Central Intelligence Agency helped to overthrow the government in 1973 and a harsh military dictatorship took control. The USA still has not solved the dilemma of keeping Communism out of its 'back yard'.

Canvas-covered missiles on the rear deck of the Soviet ship *Divinogorsk*, off Cuba in 1962.

# 10  Nuclear weapons

Several times the Western Alliance has come near to a major world war. The invention of the nuclear bomb and the perfection of the means to deliver it anywhere in the world have made the consequences of war too terrible.

The Americans used the first nuclear bomb in 1945. It was equivalent to exploding 20,000 tonnes of TNT and killed 75,000 people. So destructive was this, and a similar bomb dropped on Nagasaki a few days later, that the Japanese rapidly surrendered. So in the early days of the Cold War the USA had a monopoly of atomic weapons – until the Russians exploded their first atomic bomb in 1949.

Meanwhile the Americans were working on a

Nuclear weapon of the 'Little Boy' type, the kind detonated at Hiroshima, Japan, in the Second World War. It is three metres long.

thermo-nuclear bomb. In 1952 the hydrogen bomb was first exploded on a Pacific island with a force equal to 3.5 million tonnes of TNT (3.5 megatonnes). The Russians exploded a hydrogen bomb in 1953 and the British in 1957. These weapons have unbelievable destructive power. A 15-megatonne bomb will damage buildings up to thirty kilometres from the centre of the blast. It has been estimated that if a hundred such bombs were dropped in one day on the USA, twenty million Americans would die on the first day and twenty-two millions would perish from radiation sickness soon after.

To be effective, a country also needs to be able to deliver these bombs to their targets. Until the late

British guided weapons. This 'Thunderbird' missile lifts off during firing practice by the British Army.

51

The Vietnam War. An American plane comes in to land on the USS *America* patrolling the Tonkin Gulf.

1950s the Americans had a great lead in long range bombers which could reach deep into the USSR. During this period of American superiority the US Secretary of State, Dulles, threatened 'massive retaliation' against the Russians if they invaded the West. So the Americans were able to offset the large Communist armies in Eastern Europe. American superiority was shattered in October 1957, when the Russians launched *Sputnik*. This was the world's first artificial satellite, launched by a rocket capable of carrying a nuclear bomb from the USSR directly to targets in the USA.

The Americans feared that the Russians would, as

President Kennedy said, 'by vicious blackmail of allies' use 'sputnik diplomacy' to get their way. By the early 1960s the Americans had made a remarkable comeback. They had developed solid-fuelled ICBMs which could be stored underground. They had also perfected a method of firing an ICBM (Polaris) from a submerged nuclear submarine. These submarines cannot easily be detected, and roam the world's oceans ready to launch their missiles if the USA is attacked. Even if the United States was surprised by a Soviet nuclear attack, Americans could launch an attack which would destroy much of the USSR. The Russians too now have this capacity, and since each great power can ensure the destruction of the other even if attacked by surprise, there has been some easing of tension.

An 'Honest John' missile is launched during an exercise by the 24th Missile Regiment of the Royal Artillery.

# 11   The arms race

Nuclear weapons exist to haunt us all, but they have
not been used in a war since 1945. The same is not
true of other weapons which have been used in many
wars around the world.

The fighter aircraft is a key weapon in modern warfare. Air-to-air combat fighters now fly at more than
twice the speed of sound and have complex radar and
computer systems. Building such aircraft is so expen-

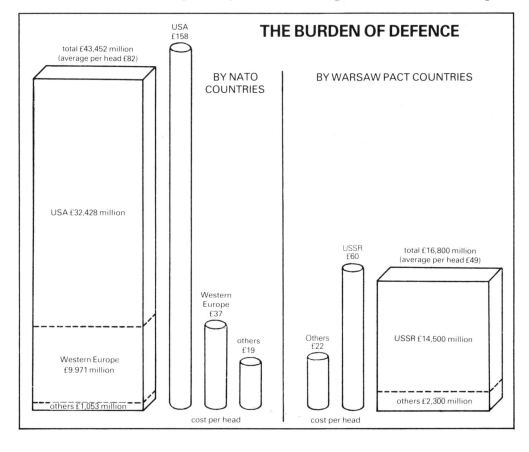

THE BURDEN OF DEFENCE

BY NATO COUNTRIES

BY WARSAW PACT COUNTRIES

total £43,452 million
(average per head £82)

USA £32,428 million

Western Europe
£9.971 million

others £1,053 million

USA
£158

Western
Europe
£37

others
£19

cost per head

USSR
£60

Others
£22

cost per head

total £16,800 million
(average per head £49)

USSR £14,500 million

others £2,300 million

sive that only the two super-powers or combinations of European nations can afford to develop them. In the early 1960s the standard American day fighter, the F100, cost $600,000 each, but one of the latest fighters, the F14A Tomcat, costs $11 millions.

A new Soviet warship of 1976, the *Kiev*, in the Mediterranean.

Another vital weapon in modern warfare is the main battle tank. Their importance has been seen in the Arab-Israeli wars. The Russians have learned from this, and their Second World War experience; they have far more heavy tanks in Eastern Europe than those available to NATO forces. These weapons cost less than modern aircraft, but Britain's new main battle tanks will each cost a million pounds.

To offset these very expensive weapons, a whole range of portable missiles have been developed. These small missiles are relatively cheap, for example the American Redeye anti-aircraft rocket costs a few thousand dollars. One might be used by a single soldier against a fighter costing millions of dollars. For this reason the poorer countries are keen to buy these weapons.

An American F-15B being refuelled in flight from a KC-135. Two other F-15's wait their turn.

The development of a whole range of military techniques by the Russians alarms the West. The Western Alliance knew for many years that the Soviet armies and tank forces were bigger than theirs. To offset this, NATO could move troops and weapons more rapidly by air and sea. This is no longer true. The expanded Soviet air transport fleet has been used to supply friendly armies in Africa and could move Soviet forces swiftly to wherever they were needed. The Soviet Navy is now so strong that it can defend the USSR coasts and also threaten the sea lanes between the USA and Western Europe. In any conventional war between NATO and the Warsaw Pact, Western Europe could not survive long if these sea lanes were cut. The Russians have also learned that in peacetime naval forces can support friends and allies and put pressure on neutral countries. Admiral Gorshkov, the creator of the modern Soviet Navy has said, 'The Soviet Navy is a powerful factor in the creation of favourable conditions for the building of Socialism and Communism.'

The many small wars, and the fears and ambitions of the great powers, ensure that enormous sums of money are spent on armaments. For example, in 1974 the USA spent about $400 on arms for every man, woman and child in the country.

*Above* A US Air Force B-52 takes off from U-Tapoa Air Base in Thailand, in October 1968.

*Left* Soviet Medium T-54 tanks, the kind used in the Arab-Israeli Six-Day War; they have 100mm guns and weigh 36 tonnes.

# 12  Disarmament and the balance of power

The cost of arms is a terrible burden. In the democratic countries of the Western Alliance, people question this burden and many think the money should be spent on social services. Communist governments are secretive about the amounts spent on arms, and their citizens have little say in the matter. But there is a limit to the amount of money that the USSR can afford to spend on arms.

There is a strong incentive for both the Western Alliance and the Warsaw Pact to try to reduce the amount spent on arms. The two super-powers, USA and USSR, also know the dangers of spreading nuclear weapons to unstable countries. There have been some successes in limiting armaments. In 1963 a partial Nuclear Test-Ban Treaty was signed after the Cuban crisis. This prohibited nuclear tests in the atmosphere and confined them underground. In 1968 in the Nuclear Non-Proliferation Treaty the USA, USSR and eighty-four other countries agreed to stop the exchange of nuclear weapons or knowledge.

Anti-aircraft ground-to-air missiles pass through Red Square on May Day.

*Above* The refugee problem. Myubi, a Baluba refugee from the Congo, and her children are to be re-housed by the UN.

*Left* US Air Force spray defoliants on Vietnamese jungle trees.

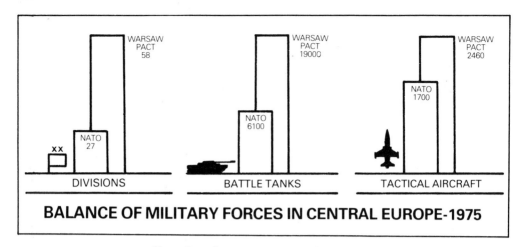

**BALANCE OF MILITARY FORCES IN CENTRAL EUROPE-1975**

Despite these treaties, those countries which wanted to enter the 'nuclear club', like France, China and India, have gone ahead and developed the weapons.

In 1972 the Strategic Arms Limitation Talks (SALT) led to an agreement by the two super-powers to limit their stocks of nuclear weapons for five years. Further SALT negotiations are going on to try to arrange more limits on missiles. But each side continued research to make their remaining missiles more effective. The Americans have developed Multiple Independently-targetted Re-entry Vehicles (MIRVs). There are a cluster of separate nuclear bombs in each ICBM, which fall accurately on dispersed targets. The Poseidon missile which carries ten MIRV warheads is replacing Polaris. The Americans have perfected the accuracy of their ICBMs. In January 1979 they announced that their missiles were aimed at Soviet missile sites and military bases and fewer on the easily-hit cities.

How do all these changes affect the vital military balance between NATO and Warsaw Pact forces in central Europe? The Warsaw Pact has far more men, tanks and tactical combat aircraft. They have standardized Soviet equipment which avoids the problems caused by the wide variety of weapons in NATO. In addition, the Warsaw Pact forces can be reinforced more quickly than can NATO forces from the USA. NATO has therefore developed a strategy of 'flexible response'. Although NATO forces cannot stop an invasion of Europe, they can use increasingly more powerful nuclear weapons as long as the Warsaw Pact forces continue to fight. In the end the Russians would have to withdraw or accept full-scale nuclear war.

# 13 The development of European unity

NATO gave Western Europe a military organization for combined defence against the USSR. It was felt that wars between Western European countries must be avoided once and for all. One way to do this was to form some kind of federal union.

In 1951 the European Coal and Steel Community was set up by France, Germany, Italy, Belgium, Netherlands and Luxembourg. France and Germany forgot their old enmity and organized an authority which could control and improve their coal and steel industries. This was a success; it was extended in 1957 when the six countries signed the Treaty of Rome to set up the European Economic Community (EEC). The members agreed that goods and workers should be allowed to move freely between them. They also agreed to work out common policies and set up authorities which would have power to take decisions affecting all the countries.

This was a major step forward towards European unity. But Britain refused to join. Britain had immense prestige at the end of the war and Churchill himself in 1946 had said 'We must build a kind of

Part of the complex of buildings used by the European Institutions in Brussels.

The centre of European economic power; the cross-shaped building is used by the permanent secretariat of the European Council of Ministers.

United States of Europe.' Yet Britain felt more involved in the affairs of her Commonwealth and Empire and in preserving the Anglo-American alliance. Britain's relations with the EEC, particularly France, became strained. Britain organized the European Free Trade Association (EFTA) in 1959 with Portugal, Switzerland, Austria and the three Scandinavian countries. This was to help trade but did not aim at political unity.

While the economic wealth of the EEC grew, Britain's economic problems increased. It seemed that Britain might recover some of her economic position if she became a member of the EEC. But when Britain applied to join the EEC in 1963 President de Gaulle of France refused. He thought Britain was an economic and military satellite of the USA and would be an American 'Trojan horse' within the EEC. The bitterness of feeling caused by this veto kept Britain out of the EEC until 1973, when the EEC was enlarged to include Britain, Ireland and Denmark.

The EEC has become one of the world's most powerful economic groupings. Its GNP is $770 billion. That of the USA is $1000 billion and USSR $500 billion. The combined population of nearly 260 million is more than that of the USA (214 million) or USSR (254 million). There are moves toward establishing a common currency, and elections for the European Parliament will be held in 1979. It is unlikely that Western Europe will become a military super-power like the USA and USSR. The economic strength of the EEC is a great asset to the Western Alliance, but the security of the West depends on joint American and European power in NATO.

# 14 Economic growth in the Eastern bloc

A government's success may be measured by the personal freedom of its people and their standard of living. Communism cannot provide the first, so must justify itself by the second. In 1949, the Russians set up the Council for Mutual Economic Assistance (usually called Comecon in the West) to give Eastern Europe what the Marshall Plan was giving the West.

For a long time Comecon was a propaganda exer-

Modern buildings in Poland. This is the church of Saint Mary the Virgin in Nowa Huta.

Modern factories are an important part of economic life in present-day Poland.

cise. Its chief purpose was to organize the economies of the satellite countries to suit the USSR. But in 1960 a new constitution was agreed, and in 1962 an executive authority was set up. Comecon could now genuinely help the whole of Eastern Europe develop in the interests of the individual countries. In particular, the Comecon countries need raw materials. Eastern European countries can rely on supplies of vital raw materials, mainly from the USSR. Oil pipelines and extensive electric grid systems have been constructed throughout the Comecon countries.

For the Russians, Comecon has a clear purpose; 'for securing the final victory in the economic competition with capitalism and ensuring the strengthening of the defensive capacity of the Comecon countries'.

How well have the Communist economies grown? When *Sputnik* was launched, Khrushchev promised that the Russian economy would overtake the American economy by 1970. It is hard to compare official statistics from Communist countries with Western ones. They ignore the very poor quality of consumer goods in the Eastern bloc and the shortages of certain services. Life is harsher with fewer luxuries than in the West. Communist economies are run from central planning offices. Officials have to decide how much each factory will produce, what prices they will charge and what wages they will pay. Trying to co-ordinate all this is too big and complex a task and grave mistakes are made which lead to shortages or waste.

Town planners ensure that factories are sited away from the modern block accommodation in Nowa Huta, Poland.

The countries in the Western Alliance are superior to those of the Communist bloc, judging only in economic terms. But there are other ways of judging success. The level of social services in the Eastern bloc is good and unemployment is rare. It is to be hoped that competition between the West and East can stay in these areas and less in the wasteful and dangerous areas of military competition.

# 15 Economic exploitation and the Third World

Most colonial countries in Asia and Africa became independent this century. But many of the new countries had unstable economies. Some relied on exports of a single agricultural crop to the former colonial power – which therefore still had economic control. Of the thirty-seven African colonies which became independent between 1960 and 1968, thirteen had declining growth rates after independence. Twelve had a per capita GNP less than $120 in 1971, when the USA per capita GNP was $5,160.

A modern industrial country can exploit the weaker countries which produce raw materials. Manufactured goods are sold at high prices in return for crops or minerals, which are often low in price. Wages are high in developed countries and low in developing countries. A good example is the trade between the USA and Latin America. Copper accounts for 73% of all Chile's exports which mainly goes to the USA or Western Europe. But when the Chilean Government

Rice farming near Samarang, Indonesia; agriculture occupies 80 per cent of the population.

Drought and primitive
farming methods in
Iran (above) and
Ethiopia (left) spell
disaster for the people.
It is to aid these people
that the UN agencies
exist.

under President Allende tried to get more benefit
from the copper mines, the USA opposed him. The
developing countries can suffer from the contact with
the richer industrial countries. Coca-Cola is sold in
the poorest countries, though for them it is an expensive drink and some of the profits go back to the USA.
Cornflakes or Weetabix advertised and sold in Kenya

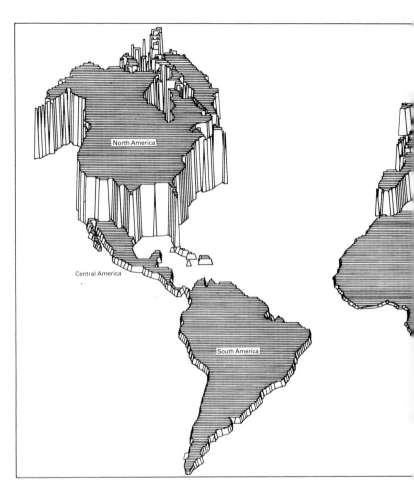

This map of the world's wealth combines the population figures and the Gross National Product of each country. The result is shown in terms of individual wealth – the higher the level of wealth, the higher the country is raised on the map.

can cost a hundred times more than the local staple foods.

Changes may be on the way. For many years the world oil market has been dominated by seven enormous oil companies. They are masters of half the world's trade and have power in many countries throughout the world. The largest is Exxon (usually known as Esso) and it is the largest company in the world, with assets worth $21,558,257,000 in 1972. Multi-national corporations have for many years extracted oil from poor countries. They pumped it into their own tankers, on to their own refineries to be sold through their own depots and filling stations. The profits flowed back mainly to the USA or Europe. The oil producing countries resented the oil com-

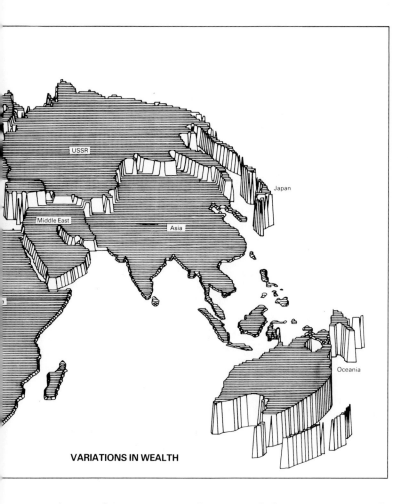

**VARIATIONS IN WEALTH**

USSR

Japan

Middle East

Asia

Oceania

panies making vast profits out of their resources. In 1960 they set up the Organization of Petroleum Exporting Countries (OPEC). This organization makes sure that the oil producing countries now get much greater profits from their oil. They act together to agree prices and force the oil companies to accept them. This has led to great increases in wealth of the oil producers, particularly in the Arab world.

Many have seen this as a threat to the industrial and economic strength of the West. But the enormous differences in wealth between the rich and poor nations of the world threaten world peace. There must be some reduction in these differences. Aid given by the developed countries is a small step in this direction.

# 16 Anti-colonialism and neutralism

A 'wind of change' swept across Africa and Asia in the twentieth century. Military and political control had been exercised by a few alien white men, who often behaved arrogantly towards the native populations, despising their cultures and religions. Westerners were superior in Asia and Africa because of their technical and scientific skills, particularly in making weapons, and their industrial knowledge. So those countries wishing to throw off European control often saw technical and industrial progress as a way to achieve it. Japan seemed a model of an Asian country which had avoided European domination by these means.

Anti-European feelings grew stronger, and European powers reacted differently in their willingness to decolonize. Generally Britain was more successful at getting out before independence movements became serious rebellions. Though in areas with military or strategic value, and only a small native population to cause trouble, there was a temptation to hold on. This happened in Cyprus, which became independent in

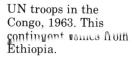
UN troops in the Congo, 1963. This contingent comes from Ethiopia.

British troops parade in Aden on the Queen's birthday in April 1961.

1960, and in Aden, which became the independent South Yemen in 1967. The French tried to hold on to their colonial possessions and fought pointless wars trying to assert their control in Indo-China and in Algeria.

The USA had always opposed European empires as unjust. After 1945, however, Americans were fighting Communism throughout the world. They lost most of their reputation as champions of the oppressed and seemed to many Asian and African people to become part of the imperialist West. The Russians and Chinese reinforced this idea with propaganda.

The newly independent countries did not want to get involved in the Cold War. Their leaders wanted to preserve their independence and raise the standard of living. The feeling developed that the Asian and African states should work together and stay neutral. In 1955, a conference of Asian and African states met at Bandung in Indonesia to assert their solidarity and neutrality. Similar conferences followed. But in the 1960s and 1970s anti-colonialism became less relevant, as all colonial control had ended. The solidarity weakened. The fear of colonial rule can still provide some unity for these states, especially because of economic exploitation. Such an enormous bloc as the African and Asian states, though, can rarely come to a united policy decision.

# 17 Nationalism

Nationalism is a belief that there should be a single, strong, independent state for people who have a powerful bond uniting them together. This bond might be a common language or religion or it might be shared experiences and history. Nationalism grew first in Europe and in its most aggressive form it reflects a feeling that the nation is superior to others and is entitled to conquer or dominate them. It was strongly felt in Nazi Germany.

It could be said that European nationalism created Asian and African nationalism by colonial rule. Asia, and more especially Africa, had different, often tribal societies which did not feel nationalism until the European conquests. It is certainly true that many of the leading nationalist figures were educated either

President Nkrumah of Ghana with Prime Minister Sir Alec Douglas-Home at No. 10 Downing Street in 1964.

in the West or were strongly influenced by Western ideas. Mahatma Gandhi, the creator of modern India, trained as a lawyer and spent part of his early life in South Africa where he grew to hate racial intolerance by white men. His great supporter, Nehru, was brought up believing in British ideas of democracy and freedom. He deeply resented the British refusal to put these ideas into practice when they ruled India. The leading nationalist in Africa was Nkrumah who led Ghana to independence in 1957. He was educated in Britain and the USA. These and other men turned their nationalism against Western rule, yet at the same time were indebted to Western ideas.

Nationalism has threatened the stability of the Western Alliance from inside. In 1958 de Gaulle became President of France and was determined to restore France's prestige and morale. It had not fully recovered after the Second World War. He disliked the way he had been treated by the British and Americans during the war and felt they still dominated the Western Alliance. He regarded partnership

Two great leaders of India. Above left, Mahatma Gandhi (1869–1948) and above right, Jawaharlal Nehru (1889–1964).

Achmad Sukarno
(1902–1970),
President of Indonesia
from 1945 to 1967,
with President Tito of
Yugoslavia.

with the USA in NATO as impossible, because: 'Everything is under the command of the Americans and [they] decide as to the use of the principal weapons – that is to say, atomic weapons.' Therefore he decided to develop a French independent nuclear deterrent, which, though extremely costly, was outside American control. In 1966 de Gaulle even withdrew France from the command structures of NATO. He asked that all NATO forces and the headquarters should be removed from France. This drastic step was loudly supported by the Russians but earned little approval elsewhere. Technically France is still a member of NATO but her withdrawal from the integrated commands has meant that in war her forces might act independently. This has weakened the Western Alliance, although since de Gaulle resigned in 1968 there are signs of France's greater willingness to co-operate in Western defence.

# 18  Limits of super-power control: Vietnam

In the 1960s the USA tried to resist Communist advance in Indo-China. This area had been under French domination but there was a strong national independence movement, led mainly by Communists under Ho Chi Minh. In 1954 they forced the withdrawal of French troops into South Vietnam. North Vietnam became an independent Communist state.

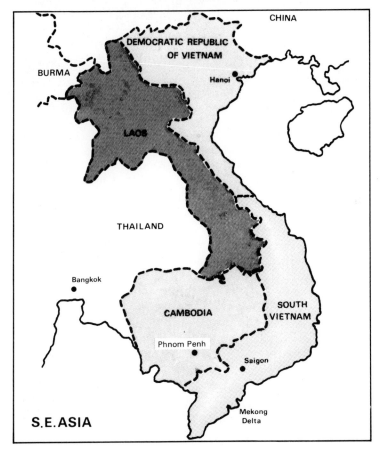

Powerful artillery of the US army, in use in Vietnam.

Laos and Cambodia became independent too, while South Vietnam, though independent, relied first on French and later American support. Soon a Communist guerrilla war broke out in South Vietnam.

The Americans saw this as an attempt by the Russians and Chinese to expand Communism in South East Asia by using the Vietcong guerrillas from North Vietnam. According to the 'domino theory', accepted by many Americans, if South Vietnam fell then Laos, Cambodia, Thailand, Burma and even India would fall in turn to the Communists. American arms, equipment and men were sent to prop up the shaky, corrupt government of South Vietnam. It became a typical guerrilla war. The Vietcong passed men and supplies down the Ho Chi Minh trail through the jungle, often on bicycles, to hide and fight in the South. They attacked American troops or supplies and then hid amongst the general population. The Americans fought back by establishing huge supply bases and strong points and attacking the enemy from the air. They also bombed military targets and communications in North Vietnam. In this effort to bomb the North Vietnamese 'back into the Stone Age' they dropped nearly seven million tons of bombs. This was almost three times as much as the bombs dropped on Germany in the Second World War.

Television showed Americans using cruel and inhuman weapons of modern war against peasants; there was widespread anti-American feeling. By 1973, the Americans had lost 56,226 men and spent well over $100,000 million. So in that year a peace agreement was signed in Paris, and the Americans withdrew most of their forces. They hoped the South Vietnamese could defend themselves. The war continued and without strong American support the South collapsed in 1975. Neighbouring Laos and Cambodia also fell under Communist governments. Once the Americans had left there was the revival of the old rivalries between Cambodia, supported by China, and Vietnam, which is supported by Russia. In 1978 Vietnam invaded Cambodia and in 1979 the Chinese invaded Vietnam. The power rivalry between Russia and China was being fought out on the battlefield.

The local population of Saigon made what profit they could from the presence of US troops during the Vietnam war.

A wounded American soldier is helped to a first aid post in Vietnam.

The Vietnam War had made the USA see the military and economic limits on its international power. This made the European members of NATO aware of the dangers of relying too much on the American nuclear 'umbrella'. Many of America's allies were very worried at the way America had abandoned South Vietnam. To make matters worse, in 1979 the USA withdrew recognition from the Chinese Nationalist government in Taiwan in favour of the Communist government in Peking.

# 19　The search for security

There have been many wars since 1945 and some of them have involved members of the Western Alliance or the Communist bloc. The leaders of the two great alliance systems, the USA and Soviet Union, have come near to war, such as in the Berlin or Cuba crises. One reason for these conflicts is the difficulty in controlling the way independent states act towards each other. It is as if within a country no police force existed and each household had to protect itself from robbers or aggressive neighbours by arming itself and relying on help from friends. One of the stronger households might act like a police force but it would

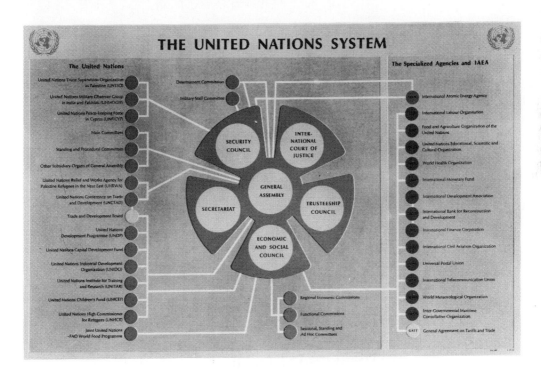

THE UNITED NATIONS SYSTEM

The Secretary-General of the UN, Kurt Waldheim, inspects the Austrian detatchment of UNDOF, in Syria.

be bound to support friends first. So the USA could never be a neutral 'world policeman.'

To deal with this kind of problem the victorious nations in the Second World War decided to set up a peacekeeping organization. The United Nations Organization (UN) began in 1945 with 51 nations and had 149 members by 1978. Each member nation is pledged to the ideal of collective security. This means that if a member state is attacked all the others would come to its aid. In such an event the Security Council would have to decide that an attack had hap-

United Nations forces in Egypt in 1974; their task was to keep peace between the Arab and Israeli armies.

pened, and that the UN should intervene. The Security Council consists of five permanent members, the USA, USSR, China, Britain and France, with fifteen non-permanent members. Since the permanent members can veto any action, it is impossible for the UN to intervene if either the USA or USSR judges that it is against their interest. Only once, in the case of Korea, did this restriction fail.

The Soviet member was boycotting the Security Council because Communist China was excluded and Nationalist China held the place.

A meeting of the General Assembly of the United Nations in New York, September 1978.

The UN has carried out a number of important and useful policing operations around the world. UN forces acted as a buffer between Egypt and Israel. They are trying to restore peace after the civil war in the Lebanon in 1979. The intervention by UN forces in Zaire involved 20,000 troops and proved to be very expensive.

As long as the great powers wish to prevent disorder they will let the UN function to restore peace within a state or between states. On the other hand they will not permit the UN to become strong enough to become a world peacekeeper, because this strength might rival their own. Also they will absolutely refuse to allow the UN to interfere in areas of vital interest to themselves. There was no UN intervention in Hungary in 1956 when the Russians put down the Nagy government, even though the Hungarians begged for such action. The UN does have useful social and economic agencies to help the poor nations but it is a failure as a means of regulating the relations between the great powers.

# 20 *Détente*

In the 1960s the Soviet leader Khrushchev evolved the policy of Peaceful Co-Existence with the West. This meant that the Russians wanted peace and cooperation while capitalism in the West was allowed to collapse through its own internal weakness.

There were various moves to bring about *détente*, a lessening of tension, throughout the late 1960s and early 1970s. In 1969 the West recognized East Germany and this reassured the USSR. Arms control treaties (see Chapter 12) depended on the two superpowers dealing with each other as equals and reach-

Strategic Arms Limitation Talks (SALT) open in Vienna in 1970. The Russian delegation is on the left and the Americans are on the right.

The symbol of *Détente*. President John Kennedy of the USA meets
Nikita Khrushchev of the USSR at Vienna in 1961.

ing agreement out of economic self interest. American and Soviet leaders visited each other's countries regularly between 1972 and 1975 and established good relations. There was a relaxation of tension, particularly in Europe.

The Chinese were very worried by these events. They felt they were now isolated; the two superpowers would take decisions which would only take account of Soviet and American interests. The Russians rejected Chinese 'unfounded rumours about "superpower collusion"'. The Chinese were pleased, however, when President Nixon visited China in 1972 to ease relations between China and the USA. Relations grew warmer when Communist China was admitted to the UN in 1971. Finally, in 1979, the USA accepted that the Communist government in Peking was the legitimate government of China. They abandoned support for the Nationalist Chinese in Taiwan. This led to a visit in February 1979 to the USA by the Chinese Vice-Premier, Deng Xiaoping. He proposed that the USA and China unite in foreign policy against the 'bullying and opportunistic polar bears' (the Russians). The Russians complained of the 'incendiary statements and the slandering of the policy of *détente*'. The Americans were rather surprised at the strength of the Chinese proposals, and had to reassure the Russians: 'Only those aspiring to dominate others have any reason to fear the further development of American-Chinese relations'.

It is clear that the Russians are disturbed by these developments. They are used to dealing with the Americans jointly to control major world crises. This 'bi-polar' world has existed because of the military balance between the two sides. The Russians now see new economic rivals in the EEC and Japan. A military alliance between the USA and China would wreck the existing military balance. This 'multi-polar' world seems to be fraught with dangers to the Russians, and some Western observers believe it might prompt them to take military action to prevent encirclement by the USA, Western Europe, China and Japan.

# 21 The future of the Western Alliance

The most obvious form of the Western Alliance is NATO. Although *détente* has reduced most of the tension in Europe, there are still dangers of conflict in many parts of the world. Western Europe is not self-contained and its trade and supplies of raw materials depend on security and peace. The turmoil in Iran in 1979 has cut off important supplies of oil. If all the Middle East oil supplies were cut off, or if they fell under the control of the Russians, Europe would be in great trouble. The Russians are openly hostile to

The Intercontinental range B-52 heavy bomber flies faster than 1,000 kph. It can hit several targets hundreds of kilometres apart on one mission.

NATO: 'The aggressive circles of NATO are the leading lights in the campaign against peace and cooperation.' The British govenment and other NATO partners feel differently: 'The comparative peace and stability which Europe has enjoyed during the past thirty years is testimony to the success of the North Atlantic Alliance.' While the world remains dangerous and international relations uncertain, it is no time to give up the collective support of NATO.

A Russian ship takes an interest in Nato exercises in the North Atlantic. In turn, it is observed by a helicopter from HMS *Ark Royal*.

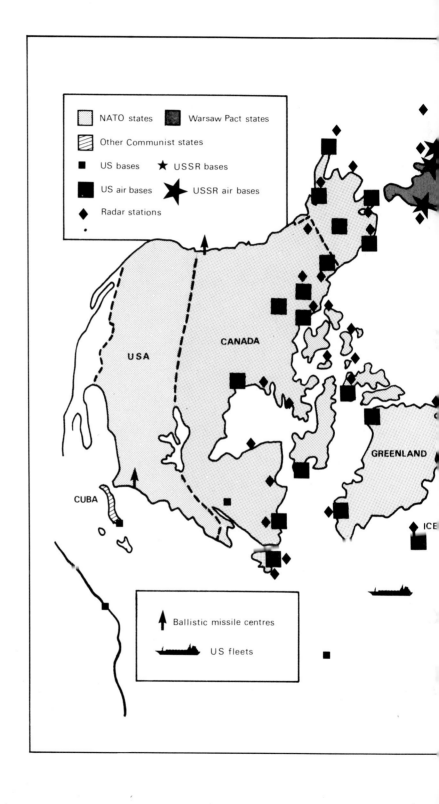

NATO states    Warsaw Pact states

Other Communist states

■ US bases    ★ USSR bases

■ US air bases    ★ USSR air bases

◆ Radar stations

USA

CANADA

GREENLAND

CUBA

ICE

↑ Ballistic missile centres

US fleets

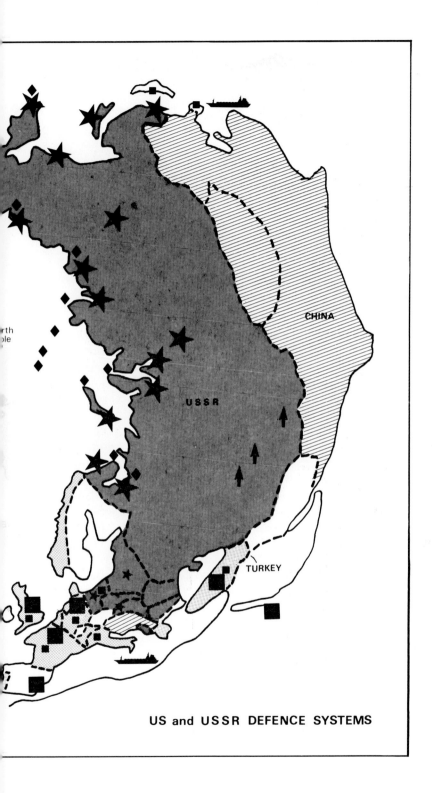

US and USSR DEFENCE SYSTEMS

The Sino-India border dispute. Chinese troops withdraw from their former positions in the Tibet region.

The Western Alliance is more than a military alliance. It is an alliance of democratic governments. They believe that citizens should have a good standard of living (which Communism also seeks) and also freedom of thought and debate. Western citizens can change their government and their political and social systems. Communists believe that they have found the right system of government, though Russians and Chinese argue about who has the true Communist system. Citizens may not change that system and are subject to control and guidance over what they should think and believe.

The West and the Communist world have many goals in common. Yet the differences are real and of great importance. There is a basic difference of view about the value of the individual human being and his right to be different and express his difference.

# Glossary

ATOMIC BOMB   A weapon which produces an explosion by splitting atoms of uranium or plutonium. It has a power between 1 and 200 kilotonnes.

BAGHDAD PACT   An alliance centred on Middle Eastern countries to link NATO and SEATO in a defence system.

BALANCE OF POWER   A stable situation where opposed nations have equal overall military strength.

CAPITALISM   An economic system based on the private ownership of property and businesses. Profits go to the owners and workers get wages for their labour.

CENTRAL INTELLIGENCE AGENCY (CIA)   American information-gathering organization which also secretly supports friendly governments and undermines enemies.

CO-EXISTENCE   Policy of Khrushchev and later Communist leaders that Communism could defeat Capitalism by peaceful means.

COLD WAR   Tension between countries where each tries to weaken the other and uses any means to do so short of actual fighting.

COLONIES   Weaker countries which are ruled by stronger countries for the strong countries' benefit.

COMECON (COUNCIL FOR MUTUAL ECONOMIC CO-OPERATION)   An economic grouping which includes the USSR, Eastern European countries and Communist countries like Cuba and Vietnam.

COMMUNISM (GENERALLY CALLED SOCIALISM IN USSR)   System where industry and businesses are owned and organized by the state. Based on the principle: 'From each according to his ability, to each according to his needs.'

CONTAINMENT American policy of stopping the spread of Communism by alliances, and war if necessary.

CONVENTIONAL WAR One in which nuclear weapons are not used.

DEMOCRACY A country ruled by an elected government which has limited powers and can be changed. Individual rights and freedoms are very important.

*DÉTENTE* A relaxation of tension between opposed countries which are suspicious of each other.

DETERRENCE A means of discouraging nuclear attack by fear of nuclear retaliation.

DEVELOPING COUNTRIES Countries without complex industrial economies. They are generally poor, and make up what is called the Third World.

DOMINO THEORY A fear that Communism will spread from one neighbouring country to another.

EAST OR EASTERN BLOC A group of Communist nations allied together to defend themselves and their political system.

GROSS NATIONAL PRODUCT (GNP) PER CAPITA The money value of all the goods and services produced in a country divided by the number of people.

GUERRILLA WARFARE War carried out by irregular soldiers within the boundaries of a country.

IDEOLOGY A group of ideas which form the basis of some economic or political system.

IMPERIALISM A policy by stronger nations to dominate weaker nations in order to secure political, military or economic advantage.

INTER CONTINENTAL BALLISTIC MISSILE (ICBM) Long range rocket which flies outside the earth's atmosphere and usually carries a nuclear warhead to its target.

IRON CURTAIN The frontier of the Eastern bloc during the Cold War which kept out people, trade and ideas from the West. The Chinese version has been called the 'bamboo curtain'.

MULTIPLE INDEPENDENTLY-TARGETTED RE-ENTRY VEHICLES (MIRV) Clusters of nuclear bombs which fall separately from one ICBM.

MULTI-POLAR WORLD One in which there are other major centres of economic or military power outside the two super-powers.

NATIONALISM   Putting the good of the state before individual needs.

NORTH ATLANTIC TREATY ORGANIZATION (NATO)   A military alliance (1949) of the USA, Canada and European countries to defend members against the USSR and its allies.

NUCLEAR WEAPONS   They use energy produced by splitting the atom in the atomic bomb or by fusion as in the much more powerful thermo-nuclear (hydrogen) bomb. They kill by blast and radiation.

POLARIS, POSEIDON   ICBMs which can be launched from a hidden, submerged submarine.

SATELLITE   A country which is so dependent on a more powerful country that it cannot have an inde-pendent policy.

SOUTH EAST ASIA TREATY ORGANISATION (SEATO)   An alliance (1954) of the USA, Euro-pean and Pacific countries to resist the advance of Chinese Communism.

SOVIET   A workers' council. Also used to describe anything to do with the USSR.

STRATEGIC ARMS LIMITATION TALKS (SALT)   Agreement between the USSR and USA to limit their stocks of nuclear weapons. A further agreement is under negotiation.

SUPER-POWER   Describes the USA and USSR because of their military and economic domination.

WARSAW PACT   The military alliance (1955) which co-ordinates the forces of the USSR and Eastern European countries.

WEST OR WESTERN ALLIANCE   A group of coun-tries, usually the NATO countries and countries with similar attitudes, determined to preserve democratic systems and individual freedoms.

# Book List

E. Barker, *The Cold War*, Wayland, 1972

C. Bown and P. Mooney, *Cold War to Détente*, Heinemann, 1976

B. Catchpole, *Map History of the Modern World*, Heinemann, 1968

P. Hastings, *The Cold War 1945–1969*, Benn, 1969

H. Higgins, *The Cold War*, Heinemann, 1974

P. Lane, *The USA in the Twentieth Century*, Batsford, 1978

P. Lane, *The USSR in the Twentieth Century*, Batsford, 1978

J. Robottom, *Making the Modern World* series, Longman, 1972

J. Robottom, *Modern Russia*, Longman, 1972

H. Ward, *World Powers in the Twentieth Century*, BBC and Heinemann, 1978

# Index

# Picture Acknowledgements

Camera Press, 21, 23, 24, 25, 26, 27, 29, 30, 34, 41, 45, 48, 52, 55, 57 (bottom), 58, 77, 86, 90; European Communities Commission, 61, 62; High Commission of India, 73 (both); Imperial War Museum, 14, 35, 50, 71; Keystone Press Agency, 10, 11, 13, 42, 43, 44, 49, 59 (bottom), 72, 74, 83, 84, 87; London Express News Service, 76, 78; Novosti Press Agency, 16, 18–19, 20; Radio Times Hulton Picture Library, 28, 39, 40; United Nations, 37, 38, 59 (top), 66, 67 (bottom), 70, 79, 80, 81, 82; US Air Force, 22, 56, 57 (top). Other pictures are from the Wayland Picture Library. Illustrations on pages 15, 32–3, 54, 60, 68–9 by Cecilia Packham-Head.